THE REMINISCENCES OF

Captain Donald O. Van Ness
U.S. Naval Reserve (Retired)

INTERVIEWED BY

Paul Stillwell

U.S. Naval Institute • Annapolis, Maryland

Copyright © 2019

Preface

In the late 1980s I set out to interview the eight then-living members of the first 13 African American line officers commissioned by the U.S. Navy. They had gone through a short training course in 1944. In the process I also interviewed white Naval Reserve officers who had been involved in the training of black sailors at segregated Camp Robert Smalls, Great Lakes, Illinois, during World War II. As I learned during the course of talking with Captain Van Ness, he had a major role in training African American recruits but did not take part in the officer training program. Thus his recollections were not included in the 1993 Naval Institute Press book *The Golden Thirteen: Recollections of the First Black Naval Officers*.

The tape has since been transcribed. Regrettably, Captain Van Ness did not have the opportunity to review the transcript during his lifetime, nor did he sign an official deed of gift. However, included in this volume is a personal letter in which he expressed his desire to be interviewed as a contribution to the historical record. In our interview he discussed the framework of training for black sailors at Great Lakes and his efforts in getting them assigned and evaluating their performance once training was completed. In 1944, while serving in the Bureau of Personnel, he made a memorable trip to the Pacific to evaluate the Navy's employment of black personnel. His naval service during World War II was a temporary interruption of his long civilian career as a businessman.

Deborah Lattimore, a long-time friend, did the excellent transcription of the original taped interview with Captain Van Ness. For their roles in collecting and preserving oral recollections, I am grateful for the support of Janis Jorgensen and Eric Mills of the Naval Institute staff. Susan Corrado of the Naval Institute Press has coordinated the printing and binding of the finished product.

Paul Stillwell
U.S. Naval Institute
October 2018

The U.S. Naval Institute Oral History Program

Researchers and authors have been drawing on the Naval Institute's Oral History Program since 1969, the year it was established by Dr. John T. Mason Jr. He and his successor, author and historian Paul Stillwell, sought to capture, preserve, and disseminate a permanent record of the stories of significant figures in naval history. In recent years, the program has expanded, with increasing numbers of historians conducting more interviews.

These oral histories are carefully fact-checked and reviewed by both historians and interview subjects before being made available. The Naval Institute is known for this high level of editorial intervention and polishing. The reader is reminded, as with all oral history interviews, that this is a record of the spoken word.

The Naval Institute wishes to acknowledge the many donors who make this program possible, in particular the generous support of the Pritzker Military Foundation of Chicago and the late Jack C. Taylor of St. Louis.

CAPTAIN DONALD OWEN VAN NESS
UNITED STATES NAVAL RESERVE (RETIRED)

Donald Van Ness was born in Paterson, New Jersey, on 4 November 1913 and attended high school in Kansas City, Missouri, where he was a colonel in ROTC. He graduated with the Naval Academy class of 1935 but was commissioned in the Naval Reserve on inactive duty because of failing eyesight. His first civilian job was as a buyer for Montgomery Ward in New York City, where he met his future wife, Marie Oropall, whom he married on 1 January 1937. He became a sales engineer for Bakelite Corporation in 1936 and in 1940 shifted to general manager of a plastic molding plant.

On 8 March 1941 Van Ness was recalled to active duty and spent the war mostly at the Bureau of Naval Personnel in Washington and at the Great Lakes Naval Training Station, Illinois. He played an important role in the development and implementation of naval plans and policies for the induction, indoctrination, and training of minorities in the Navy. At the end of the war he was assigned to Great Lakes, where he supervised the separation of officers from the Navy. He was released from active duty 31 December 1946.

On his return to inactive Naval Reserve status, Van Ness became executive vice president for the Atlas Film Corporation, and in his spare time developed a small flashing red and green light that was purchased by Quaker Oats as a cereal premium. Using his profits, he retired, bought a livestock farm in Mundelein, Illinois, became an entrepreneur and gravitated into real estate and insurance. In the next 30 years he was variously engaged in farming, real estate, insurance sales in Illinois and Western Europe, dry cleaning plants, coin-operated laundries in Chicago, laundry electronics manufacturing, a leasing company, and part ownership of a candy company.

In 1977 the Van Ness family moved to Rancho Bernardo, California, and he retired again, limiting his ownership to one dry cleaning plant and some rental properties, plus activities in the San Diego Computer Society and the American Association of Individual Investors. Sharing his wealth and expertise, he sponsored seminars on starting businesses and donated $1 million to California State University at San Marcos to support its programs for small businesses and entrepreneurs and endowed an International Institute for Entrepreneurs. The Van Nesses also became major donors to the Zoological Society of San Diego and the Sharp Hospital Foundation. He was a former member of the board of trustees of the Naval Academy Foundation. He was active in the activities of Rancho Bernardo, serving as a member of the town council, chairman of the recreation council and as a member of the planning board. He established a Naval Academy honor scholarship in memory of his classmates lost in combat.

Marie Oropall Van Ness died in 1995. The couple had no children. Captain Van Ness died on 20 October 2000 at Pomerado Hospital, California, of complications from a stroke. He was interred on 31 October 2000 with military honors at Fort Rosecrans National Cemetery in Point Loma, California. (Bio adapted from obituary in the January 2001 issue of *Shipmate* magazine.)

Don Van Ness
12664 Senda Acantilada
Rancho Bernardo, CA 92128
(619)-487-6925

November 29, 1986

Mr. Paul Stillwell
U.S. Naval Institute
Annapolis, MD 21402

Dear Mr. Stillwell:

How's this for a prompt reply to your letter of November 26 about an interview between January 12-18 in San Diego concerning blacks in the NNavy in WW II. I will be happy to meet with you.

If at all possible, you should try to visit with Charles Dillon. Between us, we ran that program from BUPERS. He now lives at 3170 Howell Rd., Golden, CO 80401. He could add a lot about Hampton Institute as well as details from BUPERS.

I will search my old files to see if I still have a copy of my report about conditions in the Pacific. For five months in 1944 I covered that area at the request of Admiral Nimitz after a race riot at Aiea Barracks in Hawaii. Old Timer's disease is beginning to set in so there's a lot I won't remember without some prodding.

My wife and I spent Thanksgiving with Alan Hemphill who is in the process of writing a book about Pete Bucher and the USS Pueblo. Alan is the one single person who probably has the most complete set of information on what happened in that case after the Pueblo was captured. He has lots of taped material that has never been made public and should have a few chapters of his book done by the time you get here. If that is in the area of your interest, I can arrange a meeting. He's an intertesting person who writes for our local paper and teaches computer science at National University. He's out of the USNA Class '57. A visit with him would be time not wasted.

My classmate, Hugh Winters, just left after spending a week with us. I had arranged a meeting between him and my dear friend, Bud Bowler, from the Institute. As a result the Institute sponsored his book entitled "Skipper" which you may have read. Bud and I got acquainted as Trustees of the USNA Foundation. It was a tragedy that he had to leave so soon.

Sincerely,

Interview with Captain Donald O. Van Ness, U.S. Naval Reserve (Retired)
Place: Captain Van Ness's home in Rancho Bernardo, California
Date: Friday, 16 January 1987

Paul Stillwell: Captain, I want to begin by expressing my pleasure at your hospitality and willingness to take part in this program and record your memories for history. Why don't we begin with a little personal background on yourself, how you came to get into the Navy, got your commission, and then what ultimately led to your involvement with the black Navy men in World War II?

Captain Van Ness: Well, I got into the Naval Academy as the result of a competitive examination in Kansas City, and I think I'd still be working on the ice truck for Kansas City Ice Company if I hadn't gotten that. It was during the Depression in 1930. When I graduated, I had bad eyes, so I didn't get a regular commission.* Ultimately I did get a commission in the reserves with a waiver, physically not qualified for sea duty. And then in March of 1941, I was recalled to active duty before the war started.

Paul Stillwell: What had you been doing in the meantime?

Captain Van Ness: In the meantime, when I first got out, I took a job as assistant buyer for Montgomery Ward in New York City, and I stayed there for about a year and then went to Bakelite Corporation, which was in the field of plastics, and up until the time I was recalled, I had stayed with Bakelite until 1940, when I went over as general manager of a plastic molding plant in Plano, Illinois, the one that actually makes the Plano fishing tackle box today. I ran that plant until March of '41, when I was recalled to active duty. So I wasn't with them very long.

Paul Stillwell: Had you gained in seniority in the reserve as these five years had passed, these six years?

Captain Van Ness: When I was recalled to active duty, I was still an ensign.

---

*Van Ness graduated in the Naval Academy on 6 June 1935. He resigned from the regular Navy on 13 September and was commissioned as a Naval Reserve ensign on 15 December 1935.

Paul Stillwell: I see.

Captain Van Ness: And I recall [chuckles] I checked in up at Great Lakes and I talked to the chief yeoman up there, who was checking us in. I said, "When does anybody get promoted in this Navy? I've been an ensign for six years." Of course, at that time you were getting $125.00 a month, so when I came back on active duty, we were kind of hit financially.

Paul Stillwell: I take it you'd been making more than that in the outside world.

Captain Van Ness: Yes, more than 125.00, right. And so this chief said, "Well, I think what you ought to do is put in a request to be promoted." [chuckles]

"Well," I said, "Chief, now, don't pull my leg." I said, "I never thought of anybody putting in a request to be promoted."

"No," he said, "that's right." And he brought out an AlNav that showed how you put in a request to be promoted.*

So at lunch, I went out and I met with some of the other fellows that came in at the same time, and there was a fellow there who had been an ensign for 11 years, Red Edwards. [laughter] I said, "Red, you know, you're the bull ensign on the station here. Why don't you put in a request to be promoted?" Well, he almost fell off the chair, you know, laughing at the idea of putting in a request. I said, "Well, that's what the chief told me to do, and I'm gonna do it."

So I put in the request to be promoted, and, by God, in about a couple of months, I was promoted to lieutenant (junior grade) and he was still an ensign. [laughter] And I, from then on, was promoted ahead of him all during the war.

Paul Stillwell: Did you ever catch up to your class in promotions?

Captain Van Ness: No. In May of '44, we had a race riot out at Aiea Barracks in Hawaii, and Admiral Nimitz wanted somebody to come on out there, look into it, because he was concerned about what problems might result from that. Captain Tommy Darden was the chief of planning for the Chief of Bureau of Naval Personnel, and he selected me to go on out there to cover the Pacific and hit these different places where the blacks were, and find out just what was going on.†

---

* AlNav is a type of message put out to all the Navy.
† Captain Thomas F. Darden Jr., USN.

At that time, I was a lieutenant commander. He said, "To make your job a little easier we're going to give you a spot promotion to commander."

Well, a couple, three days later, he came to me and he said, "I feel badly about this, but if we do this, we're going to put you ahead of your classmates." [laughs] So I didn't get the spot promotion, and rightfully so. They were out there in the shooting war, and I was in Washington. So I didn't get promoted to commander until the day the war ended. The medical officer was signing the papers when it came over the radio the war was ended.

Paul Stillwell: Well, you probably were pretty close to caught up with them then, because they were commanders, too, at that point.

Captain Van Ness: Yes, but they were commanders ahead of me. I made captain in '56, and I don't know when my class made captain. I have no idea.

Paul Stillwell: Was Great Lakes your initial duty assignment then?

Captain Van Ness: Yes, I was put into recruit training, and I remember checking in there.[*] Roger Nelson was his name, the commander who had charge of recruit training.[†] I had reported in on a Sunday, and I wasn't happy about being recalled back to active duty. First place, I knew there wasn't going to be a war, and it was just one of those things that they were going to build up the Navy and all that.

Paul Stillwell: So you were recalled before Pearl Harbor.[‡]

Captain Van Ness: Right. March of '41. And I went to the officers' club on Sunday night, and there, unfortunately, ran into the station drunk at the bar, stayed with him. We went out to dinner together, and he brought me back that night. We stayed in what they called the guinea Pullman, which was some portion of the officers' club, and that's where you slept. Well, I didn't know

---

[*] Recruit training, known more commonly as boot camp, was conducted at the Naval Training Station, Great Lakes, Illinois, about 30 miles north of downtown Chicago on the shore of Lake Michigan.
[†] Lieutenant Commander Roger E. Nelson, USN.

[‡] On Sunday, 7 December 1941, Japanese carrier planes attacked and heavily damaged American warships at the naval base at Pearl Harbor, Hawaii. The U.S. Congress declared war on Japan the following day.

there was anybody else down there sleeping. We went on down, and he was a dental officer and was living it up, and he was bellowing and making a lot of noise, and all of a sudden, out of the dark, some voice says, "Damn it, don't you know there's people trying to sleep here?" So he got out and left me there. [laughter]

The next morning, I got up, and I'm in there brushing my teeth, and in comes this gray-haired fellow. Well, I knew right away he wasn't an ensign. [laughter] He started turning to me and said, "Was that you came in last night, made all that noise?"

I said, "Well, I don't know as I was making any noise, but, yeah, I did come in late last night."

Well, the first guy that I had to report to was this same officer, Jim—it doesn't matter. Had to report to him. [laughs] So he had a kind of smirk on his face when I checked in that morning. He sent me down to recruit training. There was a fellow by the name of Roger Nelson, was the commander, and he had charge of recruit training. I came in, "Ensign Van Ness, reporting for duty, sir."

He looked up at me, great big bushy eyebrows. He said, "Are you a regular or reserve?"

I said, "I'm a reserve, sir."

"Goddamn it, we ask for men and all we get's reserves." [laughter] So I was ready to go home right then and there.

Mrs. Van Ness: Made your day, didn't it?

Captain Van Ness: But they assigned me to recruit training, and I stayed with that, had a battalion and then eventually had a regiment. Then I think it was in May of '42 when they started taking in blacks for general service.*

Paul Stillwell: Had there been blacks there before?

Captain Van Ness: Yes, as steward's mates. And there were blacks who had general service ratings, but very few of them. I mean, there were some machinist's mates and things like that that we had in the Navy, who had come up through the ranks. Now, when they got that, I don't recall, because it was not a general practice to take them in, except as steward's mates.

---

* The change that permitted entry by black enlisted men into the Navy's general service ratings became effective in June 1942. Until then they had been limited almost exclusively to duty as cooks and stewards, that is, servants to officers.

Paul Stillwell: Had they perhaps started as steward's mates and then converted?

Captain Van Ness: I don't know. I probably knew at that time and I don't recall now.

So they opened up this camp—they called it Camp Robert Smalls—and put me over in charge of the camp.* Prior to that, a man by the name of Dan Armstrong came in, and he had quite a bit of knowledge about the blacks.† I think it started back with his dad, who had done work with the blacks in the South. I thought he was a very capable guy and with a lot of imagination, and because of the job that he had, there were a lot of officers that didn't like him, not because he was Dan Armstrong, I think, but mostly because of what he was working on. There was a natural resentment that existed among naval officers; they didn't want blacks and they particularly didn't want black officers.

Paul Stillwell: Perhaps before we get completely into that, you could comment on the build-up that occurred at Great Lakes as these vast hordes of men came in to be trained.

Captain Van Ness: Yes. As a matter of fact, I was taken from my battalion and made assistant to a lieutenant by the name of Bill Turek, who had the receiving unit where everybody was coming in.‡ It was particularly bad right after December 7. I mean, they were tearing the gates down to get on active duty. It wasn't like it was in Vietnam or any other war since. I mean, there was a great support for getting in, fighting the Japanese and whatever.

Paul Stillwell: Was there a lot of construction of facilities?

** Within the Great Lakes Naval Training Station, Camp Robert Smalls was the site of training for black recruits. It was named for an escaped slave who captured the Confederate steamer *Planter* during the Civil War and turned her over to the U.S. Navy. He served as pilot of the *Planter* and later of the gunboat *Keokuk*. After the war, Smalls (1839-1915) served in the U.S. Congress as a representative from South Carolina from 1875 to 1879 and from 1884 to 1887.

† Commander Daniel W. Armstrong, USNR, was officer in charge of Camp Robert Smalls. A 1915 graduate of the Naval Academy, he resigned his regular commission in 1919 to pursue a civilian career. He was recalled to active duty for World War II, serving at Great Lakes and in the Pacific theater. Daniel Armstrong (1893-1947) was the son of Civil War Union General Samuel Chapman Armstrong, who founded Hampton Institute in Virginia in 1868 as a trade school for black students. Daniel Armstrong was born the same year his father died.

‡ Lieutenant William Turek, USNR.

Captain Van Ness: The whole golf course that was there—everything was taken over and they started building barracks. They built them so fast that they didn't even get the proper heating facilities established by the time the men got there. I can remember in the winter there of '41, where people were sleeping in barracks, there was no heat, and sleeping in hammocks when the temperature got down way low as it does up around Chicago. They had little what they called salamanders, where they were heating the barracks, which was kind of a little portable stove, and didn't do much of a job of heating.

So they were expanding very rapidly, bringing in—I can't recall how fast they were coming in, but we ended up we had about 100,000 people at Great Lakes, not all of them recruits, but the majority of them were recruits. And of that group, my regiment was about 5,000. When they started to bring the blacks in, they assigned me over to the job to take over this first regiment, and we ultimately had 5,000 in that regiment.

The bad parts—and I think I ought to tell this—that would be roughly about 5% of the station, and I had over 50% of the venereal disease of the station. I had I don't know what percentage, but a great majority of the knifing cases on station. So we had many problems there at the beginning.

Another thing was that a lot of them were illiterate, and we had to start a remedial training program to teach them to read.

Paul Stillwell: Were there such programs for the white sailors also?

Captain Van Ness: Not to my knowledge. We didn't have them in my other white regiment. I don't know of any others that had it. I think we were the only ones that started that remedial program.

Paul Stillwell: How did you happen to get involved in the program at Robert Smalls?

Captain Van Ness: Well, by that time, I think—I don't remember who was recruit training officer, but Bill Turek, who was my immediate superior, was asked to recommend somebody to take over the regiment, and he's the one that recommended me.

Paul Stillwell: Did you have any reluctance or hesitation about that?

Captain Van Ness: No.

Paul Stillwell: I would imagine there were some who would have had.

Captain Van Ness: I think that perhaps that might have been true, particularly if they had been regular Navy. I think more so the regular Navy might have been more reluctant to have that job, but that's only—I'm not sure that that's a true statement.

Paul Stillwell: Well, but you've talked about these people who didn't like Armstrong for being involved, so presumably they would not have wanted to have been involved personally.

Captain Van Ness: My feeling is based on that, really.

Paul Stillwell: What kind of a person was Armstrong?

Captain Van Ness: Well, I thought he was a very energetic and dynamic type of guy, with lots of imagination, lots of ideas. He wasn't the bureaucratic type, you know, that worried a lot about paperwork and what the book said. His goal—and I might say mine too—was to get the job done, and to hell with what the book said. We actually did things that maybe shouldn't have been done, but in order to get the job completed, you had to change things.

Paul Stillwell: What might be examples of going against the book?

Captain Van Ness: Well, today I would probably be court-martialed for some of the things that I did.

Paul Stillwell: Well, I think the statute of limitations has expired. [laughter]

Captain Van Ness: And not only that, I'm retired now. But, for example, something had to be done about those things that I cited, the knifing cases. You couldn't just say, "Well, we've got a lot of knifing cases. So what? What can we do about it?" I started a program to train people that if they had arguments, to settle them in the boxing ring or talk it over or whatever, but not to pull knives on one another. It didn't do much good. They still kept doing it.

So I had a black there, whose name I don't recall, who was a sparring partner of Joe

Louis.[*] I called him in and asked him if he would conduct a training program for anybody who pulled a knife on anybody else that was reported. Then we would bring him into the drill hall and lay down a mat, and brought his company in to surround the mat, and then this guy was to give him boxing instructions. I told him to give him enough instructions that by the time he left, he would remember [chuckles] not to pull a knife. And that was very effective. It didn't eliminate knife-pulling, but it made it drop down considerably, because nobody wanted to get in the ring with this fellow.

Paul Stillwell: So his instruction involved beating them up, essentially. [laughter]

Captain Van Ness: In a sense, yeah. Now, today you'd be in trouble for doing that.

Mrs. Van Ness: Well, they wore boxing gloves.

Captain Van Ness: Again, the point is that it got results. It made them aware right away that pulling a knife wasn't the way to solve a problem.

Paul Stillwell: How did you go about attacking the venereal disease problem?

Captain Van Ness: We put prophylactic boxes in the barracks, and even there, it was reported to the commanding officer of the station, who was a captain, by the chaplains that I was promoting immorality. So I was called up, and I explained the problem, and the commanding officer said, "You just go right ahead."

Paul Stillwell: Well, that was pretty much Navy policy, though, wasn't it?

Captain Van Ness: No, we didn't have those things in the barracks.

Paul Stillwell: What about if a guy came down with the disease? Then was he restricted?

---

[*] Joseph Louis Barrow (1914-1981) was a black boxer who fought under the name Joe Louis. He won the boxing heavyweight title in 1937 and successfully defended the title 25 times before retiring in 1949. A later comeback failed. In June 1936, before becoming champion, Louis lost to German fighter Max Schmeling, then avenged that loss with a first-round knockout of Schmeling in June 1938.

Captain Van Ness: I don't remember exactly what happened. Of course, they were restricted anyhow, you know, during the recruit training. I don't recall how soon we would let them out to go on weekend leave. I don't recall now. Time has made me forget a lot of these things.

Paul Stillwell: Well, they sure weren't catching the VD in the barracks. [laughs]

Captain Van Ness: No, no, that's right. [laughter] But I don't know. We had a big reception center there at our camp, and I don't want to go into detail, but [chuckles] they would find ways to—and their girlfriends could come in, you see, and visit with them in this recreation center, and people can become very imaginative about how they get around getting involved in things like that.

Paul Stillwell: Well, they must have got liberty at some point after they'd been there a while.

Captain Van Ness: Yes. I don't remember when it was. I don't remember anymore.

Paul Stillwell: How did you go about selecting the instructors and the chief petty officers for the individual companies?

Captain Van Ness: We had a policy that we didn't want castoffs from other places, and it was a base policy. The commanding officer of the station felt the responsibility that this was something that was a touchy thing, it was something new to them, and they were afraid of criticism on both sides, white and black, so they wanted to get the best quality of petty officers that they could get. A large percentage of those that we did get were what they called the "Tunney Fish." You know the Gene Tunney program brought in athletes, and they became chiefs and did an excellent job too.[*]

Paul Stillwell: So these were not necessarily career Navy men.

Captain Van Ness: No, no. No, they weren't. But most of them were college graduates and fine people, and I thought did an excellent job.

---

[*] Lieutenant Commander James J. "Gene" Tunney, USNR, had been the heavyweight boxing champion from 1926 to 1928. During World War II, he was in charge of the Navy's program of athletic instruction. The men he recruited as assistants were given direct appointments as chief petty officer specialists.

Paul Stillwell: Well, they would deal with the physical training, but you must have had some—

Captain Van Ness: No, they were the company commanders.

Paul Stillwell: Oh, really?

Captain Van Ness: Yes, they were the chiefs who took over and did the training, the drilling and seamanship and all that. Of course, we would have people who were particularly well qualified in certain subjects, you know, to take charge of that particular subject, like seamanship and so on.

Paul Stillwell: Well, who would those people be? Were they experienced Navy men?

Captain Van Ness: Some were, and some were the Gene Tunney men.

Paul Stillwell: Then you must have had some sort of program to train the Tunney people so they could then train the recruits.

Captain Van Ness: Well, for example, I had a warrant officer that had been a chief boatswain's mate, and they would run classes for our own people to help them out in the training of the recruits, you know, when they got into technical subjects. In fact, the fellow that did our swimming instruction, he later became governor of the state of Illinois, Haller.*

Paul Stillwell: Well, what about the marching and drilling aspects? Did you teach that to the Tunney people?

Captain Van Ness: Yes. Now, I learned one thing early in the game, that the blacks, in general, at that time, at least the upper echelon—we were visited quite often by people from the National Association of Colored People and Urban League and so on—they didn't like to hear things, that the blacks were good at marching, blacks were good at singing, that sort of thing.

Paul Stillwell: The stereotypes.

---

* Daniel J. Walker served as governor of Illinois from 8 January 1973 to 10 January 1977. He was a Navy enlisted man before entering the Naval Academy in 1942. His profile does not fit the individual Van Ness described.

Captain Van Ness: Yeah. But as a matter of fact, they *were* good at marching.

Paul Stillwell: Better as a group than the whites?

Captain Van Ness: I would say yes.

Paul Stillwell: Did you have some sort of screening program to determine that the people who were assigned to the black boot camp would be sympathetic and supportive of the blacks' cause?

Captain Van Ness: I don't know. I didn't have the job of selecting the people that came in.

Paul Stillwell: Who was that?

Captain Van Ness: That was Bill Turek, the recruit training officer. But I do know that they were conscientiously trying to get good people. They wanted to make the program work. Whether or not they were interested in blacks in the Navy, I can't say, but they wanted to make the program work because the spotlight was on them, and the CO of the station said, "I want this thing to be run without any problems." First place, it was a Jim Crow camp, all black, see, except for the petty officers, and we had black petty officers, too, of the old Navy, but it was a Jim Crow camp.[*]

I do recall that when I was in Washington, Truman Gibson was the man in the Army who had charge of the black program, and he was black, a very light-colored black, and a very good man, I mean knowledgeable and presentable.[†] We used to have lunch together quite often, talk about our particular problems. He was very much opposed to the Jim Crow camp that we had, and I told him that I understood his feelings, but I said, "Have you ever been down in the camp? Have you ever had a regiment of these people yourself?" No, he hadn't.

I said the difference is that when you're down there, you see what the real problems are, and there is a tenseness about bringing blacks into the Navy, and if we didn't have a Jim Crow camp where we could teach them how to do the proper thing, just like no knifing and taking a shower and keeping your clothes rolled properly and all the neatness and cleanliness. I know from actual experience that they were not the type that would do all the things that they were supposed

---

[*] Thomas D. Rice, a black minstrel singer, wrote a song and dance titled "Jim Crow" in 1832. Later in the century, the term took on the meaning of segregation of the races, as in "Jim Crow laws."
[†] During World War II Truman K. Gibson, an attorney, served as advisor to Secretary of War Henry L. Stimson on racial matters.

to do, and if they were mixed with the whites, it would only prove that the whites were right, that they were not up to the caliber that the Navy wants. So we had to put them through a program to teach them the things that they didn't know when they came in.

Paul Stillwell: Well, but presumably a lot of whites had to be taught those same things.

Captain Van Ness: I know, but whites can understand some other white who doesn't come up to par, but it would be very easy for them to grab on and make a stereotype out of all blacks, because, as a matter of fact, there were a higher percentage of blacks who didn't keep clean and didn't do the things that whites generally do in everyday living. So it would have only made it more difficult, in my opinion, if we had integrated them immediately. Today there's integration and there's not any problem that I'm aware of, but I'm not close to it anymore. I don't know.

Paul Stillwell: Was there a specific effort to keep white men from being involved in Camp Robert Smalls who were known to be prejudiced or opposed to blacks?

Captain Van Ness: I don't recall having found anybody who wasn't willing to work with the blacks, but if we had found them, we would have transferred them some other place.

Paul Stillwell: Certainly wouldn't have forced them into it.

Captain Van Ness: No, no. No, no.

Paul Stillwell: So you were convinced it was a good-faith effort to give the blacks training, to get them into the Navy?

Captain Van Ness: Yes.

Paul Stillwell: What was your perspective, from the regimental level, in the operation of Camp Robert Smalls?

Captain Van Ness: From what angle?

Paul Stillwell: Well, what were your specific duties in seeing that the men were trained?

Captain Van Ness: Well, I guess the same as it would have been in any regiment, just to make sure that, you know, you'd have meetings with your officers in setting up a program of—we used the same basic training procedures that we did for the whites, and we tried to develop an enthusiasm for what the instructors were doing, and I really feel that they all conscientiously did a good job.

Paul Stillwell: Did you feel that the black recruits were embracing this enthusiastically, seeking to pick up the knowledge and get on with their part in the war?

Captain Van Ness: I would say that they weren't much difference than my experience with the whites in that regard. They were in there, just as a lot of whites were—you know, after the first furor of beating down the gates, "Let's get in," a lot of people came in that weren't happy about coming in, particularly older ones who were pulled away from jobs, I think up to age 38, you know, being drafted. But none of us—I wasn't happy when I was recalled either, but after the war started, I mean, your attitude changed. It was something had to be done.

Paul Stillwell: Did you get involved in personnel inspections and barracks inspections?

Captain Van Ness: Yes.

Paul Stillwell: What do you recall about those?

Captain Van Ness: Well, I would say that after the first couple of weeks, they shaped up. If they didn't shape up, there was a lot of extra duty and restrictions and discipline that would make them want to shape up.

Paul Stillwell: Well, that's the negative part of it, the carrot-and-stick approach. There must be people who are motivated by the desire to win awards and praise and that sort of thing too.

Captain Van Ness: Well, we did that because we had competition very similar to a program in the white camps. We had the "E" awards for the outstanding companies, and there was a real competition, not just within the recruits, but among the chiefs. They were in the spirit of things too. They liked to have their company win the award.

Paul Stillwell: Were you a jaygee when you were starting to work in this program with the blacks?* Did you have any officers working for you?

Captain Van Ness: Let's see. By then, I think I had been promoted to lieutenant, I believe. I'm not sure.

Paul Stillwell: Did you have any officers working for you?

Captain Van Ness: Oh, yeah. Each battalion had an officer.

Paul Stillwell: Do you recall the names of any of those?

Captain Van Ness: Paul Richmond was one; John Dille.†

Paul Stillwell: I've talked to Dille.‡

Captain Van Ness: Yeah. And a fellow by the name of Kauffold.§

Paul Stillwell: Dille was in the same category as you for physical reasons. He was not eligible for sea duty. He had colorblindness.

Captain Van Ness: I don't remember. He was a very good officer, though. All of them were. All of them were above average for their rank, I would say.

Paul Stillwell: I wonder if it was true of them generally that these were men who, for physical reasons, were not qualified for sea duty, and that's why they were there.

---

* Jaygee – lieutenant (junior grade).
† Ensign Paul D. Richmond, USNR, graduated from the Naval Academy in December 1941, but vision problems prevented him from serving at sea. He was assigned to Great Lakes and in 1944, as a lieutenant (junior grade) devised the curriculum that was used in training the Golden Thirteen, the Navy's first black line officers. Richmond's oral history is in the Naval Institute collection.

‡ Lieutenant (junior grade) John F. Dille Jr., USNR. His oral history is in the Naval Institute collection.
§ Ensign Vance A. Kauffold, USNR.

Captain Van Ness: If that was the case, I wasn't aware of it.

Paul Stillwell: What specifically do you remember about Dille?

Captain Van Ness: Well, like I said, he was a good officer, took his job seriously, and took a real interest in the recruits and did his best to help them, you know, conscientious.

Paul Stillwell: How much direct contact did you have with the black recruits?

Captain Van Ness: Myself?

Paul Stillwell: Yes.

Captain Van Ness: Not a lot. In other words, the battalion commander is the one that did it, but I would come around for inspections. I would take the reviews and present awards, things like that were where I got involved. And in the general administration of the regiment, I mean, there was a lot of work involved there. You're not just sitting behind a desk. In fact, there were many long hours. I used to go back to the camp at night, you know, go around, see what the guards were doing, things like that, to make yourself visible and let them know that the thing was serious.

Paul Stillwell: What sorts of methods did you have for evaluating progress and seeing that the training was being carried out and the men were performing well?

Captain Van Ness: Well, mostly by observation. We had testing programs for the recruits. Most of the things were administered by the battalion commanders themselves. They had a schedule to follow. In other words, at certain hours we had scheduled certain things and it was on a great big thing, and that I drew up myself. That was one of the things that I set up first in order to coordinate the use of the facilities that we had and keep them in use all the time without conflict between two companies going to the same place at the same time.

Paul Stillwell: How much was physical training part of the overall program?

Captain Van Ness: Oh, I don't remember, but we had a lot of it, a lot of physical training, and we had a lot of sports, so that was all mixed in with the regular technical training, you know, learning plane recognition, seamanship, and learning how to use the rifle and so on.

Paul Stillwell: And along with those military subjects, you were also instilling a sense of naval discipline.

Captain Van Ness: Yes.

Paul Stillwell: Inevitably, there are some people who just can't adjust to that or who can't make the mustard academically. How did you deal with those cases?

Captain Van Ness: Well, the remedial school, if there was a problem along that line, was the first thing we gave them, and that was done after hours, you know. You had to go to the remedial school. And I think that they were interested in trying to learn how to read and write better.

Paul Stillwell: Did you have a fair degree of success with that school?

Captain Van Ness: You know, I don't really know how successful we were. I know they learned something while they were going through there. How much, I can't really say. I really don't know how successful we were. I know they improved. Beyond that, I can't really say.

Paul Stillwell: One of the first black officers, Dennis Nelson, was involved in that program.* Do you have any memories of him?

Captain Van Ness: Just the name. As I recall, he was one of the lighter-colored officers, too, if I remember correctly, but I don't remember a lot about him. We used the blacks as much as possible for a lot of those things, because we felt that they had a better understanding and perhaps

---

* Ensign Dennis Denmark Nelson II, USNR, was a member of the Golden Thirteen. He eventually retired from the Navy as a lieutenant commander. He died in 1979 before he could be interviewed as part of the Naval Institute's oral history program. Nelson's master's thesis was published by the Navy Department in 1948 and later came out as a book, *The Integration of the Negro into the U.S. Navy* (New York: Farrar, Strauss and Young, 1951).

would get a better response from the recruits than maybe some of the whites might have. That was just a theory. I don't know whether that's true or not.

Paul Stillwell: Possibly a better rapport.

Captain Van Ness: Yes, that I'm sure of. They would be more honest with each other perhaps.

Paul Stillwell: Well, but there wouldn't be the race barrier to overcome.

Captain Van Ness: That's what I mean. They would say things, the way they talk among themselves, that they might not say if they had a white there with them.

Paul Stillwell: Be less on guard, probably.

Captain Van Ness: Yeah.

Paul Stillwell: Did you get involved in the officer training program?

Captain Van Ness: No.

Paul Stillwell: How much aware of that were you as it was going on?

Captain Van Ness: Not too much, and I didn't have much in the way of selection. Dan Armstrong was pretty much responsible for that. Of course, I did give him my recommendations, you see. By that time, we had two regiments of blacks. I believe there were two then. But I didn't have anything to do with the officer training part of it, other than nominating people, but Dan was the one who made the final selections.

Paul Stillwell: Did the numbers of blacks at Camp Robert Smalls increase as the build-up went on for the war effort?

Captain Van Ness: I think it was two regiments we had. I really can't recall now for sure, but I think it was just two. [unclear] Camp Robert Smalls and then eventually had another regiment.

Paul Stillwell: How long did you stay there at Great Lakes with that program?

Captain Van Ness: That was until—let's see. I can't remember whether it was September of '42 or '43. I guess it was '43 that I was ordered to BuPers.[*]

Paul Stillwell: So you were there two-plus years involved in the recruit training.

Captain Van Ness: Uh-huh.

Paul Stillwell: What changes did you see over that time?

Captain Van Ness: Well—

Paul Stillwell: Presumably you learn from mistakes and you get better as you go along.

Captain Van Ness: Yes. Well, that's how, you know, you develop the remedial program, you develop the boxing instruction program, you know. Things just sort of evolved as you went along. You found that you needed something that you weren't aware of, or some chief would come up and say, "I think we ought to do so-and-so." Things like that would be tried, because they were working closely with the men, and they would know how the men were reacting to things.

Paul Stillwell: Do you have any specific memories of things?

Captain Van Ness: No, no, not now.

Paul Stillwell: What recreational facilities were there for the recruits?

Captain Van Ness: Well, we had our own swimming pool, we had our own recreation building. They were exactly the same as all the other camps had. We had good facilities, as good as could be provided, you know, at a time like that. I don't think there was any complaint from anyone about what was provided for them.

---

[*] BuPers – Bureau of Naval Personnel, then located in Arlington, Virginia.

Paul Stillwell: Inevitably, you have some people who have a problem adjusting. They're away from home, they're in this strange environment. Were there chaplains there that they could be counseled?

Captain Van Ness: Yes. We had a chaplain, a Chaplain Flowers [phonetic], and there was another one whose name I can't remember. Chaplain Flowers, as I recall, was from Alabama, a very good officer, good chaplain, very conscientious, and we called on him for help on occasions, because they would sit down and talk with the chaplain more than they would with the line officers about certain things.

Paul Stillwell: How much interest was there from the news media in the training of black sailors?

Captain Van Ness: A fair amount, more so than there was with whites, for example. But a lot of it was concentrated with the black newspapers, and we cooperated with them. The black papers were always inclined to be on the critical side, but I suppose they were just about the same as the white newspapers, always looking for something to pick on, real or imagined.

Paul Stillwell: What sorts of things did they criticize?

Captain Van Ness: Primarily the Jim Crow aspect of it, which is true. I mean, it was definitely a Jim Crow camp, but you heard how I rationalize why it was a good thing at the time. When they got out, today's system is much better.

Paul Stillwell: Did you provide that explanation to them at the time?

Captain Van Ness: No. Oh, the newspapers?

Paul Stillwell: Yes, the reason for the separation.

Captain Van Ness: Well, every once in a while, I would read the black papers, but I didn't want to—you don't get very far telling things like it is all the time. It's hard to tell a black newspaper reporter that, "We've got these problems with blacks that we don't have with whites," you know.

Paul Stillwell: Well, how did you deal with their questions then?

Captain Van Ness: Well [chuckles], I would tell them, "We've got a pretty high venereal disease rate." Well, they wouldn't put that in the paper. "And we have the most knifing cases." Well, that didn't go in the paper either. Things like that didn't get in the black paper, but you had the Jim Crow situation, that got in the paper and, you know, was criticized. And I can understand how they would feel, but they weren't looking at it, in my opinion, from the standpoint of what good it was going to do the Navy or the blacks, ultimately. That was their policy: "We're against Jim Crowism." And I think if I were black, I'd feel the same way.

Paul Stillwell: Well, but you cited these two things, the knifings and the VD, as the reason for the separation?

Captain Van Ness: And their performance was not up to the performance of the whites. This I could say because I had white regiments, too, you see.

Paul Stillwell: Performance measured how?

Captain Van Ness: Well, conduct, you know, name-calling. Not that they don't have name-calling in whites, but I mean they had the strangest kinds of name-calling that I don't want to go into, you know, things that you'd be repulsed if a white group were to say. They had their own type of language, and some of it was pretty raw. The things I've already stated: venereal.

Paul Stillwell: Well, but performance goes to more substantial things like that, like performance on tests and competitive exercises.

Captain Van Ness: But they, you know, would be down at the bottom of the heap. Just recently in the newspaper, for example, you heard or read that the American schools were down at the bottom of the heap as far as mathematics, and they compared them with the schools in a certain town in Japan and Taipei in Taiwan and so on. But they compared them with schools in Chicago! Now, there's a *high* percentage of blacks in the schools in Chicago, and I'm sure that those schools in Chicago have the same problem that we had, that they were not up to par education-wise. So, to me, it wasn't a good comparison.

Paul Stillwell: But you'd say across the board, the white regiments performed better than the blacks?

Captain Van Ness: Yes.

Paul Stillwell: How was the spotlight of attention manifested that you spoke of, in seeing that the black programs were successful? Did you have visits from Washington, for example?

Captain Van Ness: There were both black and white visitors, you know, coming in, because it was new. People wanted to know how they were doing. And when we had a review, I think we did an excellent job with anything along that line. It was in the technical aspects, the things that required some kind of educational background, where we fell down, and when I say that, that doesn't mean that all of them are that way. We had some that were topnotch people. It's just that we had too many who weren't.

Paul Stillwell: Was there a concern on the part of the black media and these visitors and so forth to ensure that the facilities and training and conditions were the same in Camp Robert Smalls as they were on the main side, white recruits?

Captain Van Ness: I don't recall of any criticism from any of those groups because of that.

Paul Stillwell: But was that an item of concern with them?

Captain Van Ness: Apparently it was, but we would always—I would personally take these visitors around to let them see what was going on, where they could see the training and the facilities and where they lived, to help dispel any of that fear that they might have.

Paul Stillwell: You spoke of the critical aspects of the black papers. They would understandably be critical of the Jim Crow, but I think a positive in publicizing the achievements of blacks' performance in the boot camp.

Captain Van Ness: Well, you know, it's been so long ago, if you try to pin me down, I can't be specific because I can't remember. You know, I have this general feeling that they were critical all the time, and they were, but if you ask me about what, I can't remember enough of it.

Paul Stillwell: That's an interesting perception, because I've seen the scrapbooks of some of the early black officers, and they're filled with these stories about black Navy men who were top of their company or whatever achievement they had in Robert Smalls.

Captain Van Ness: Well, and we played that up all the time. It was a morale factor, and whenever anybody did anything outstanding or did it well, we wanted to play that up as a role model for the rest of them. That's what I say. They weren't all slobs, you know. We had some good people.

Paul Stillwell: What was your technique in publicizing the role models?

DVN: Well, of course, like you say, it got in the papers, and the newspapers were always watching everything. If I remember right, I think Dille was doing a lot of the PR.

Mrs. Van Ness: He was.

Paul Stillwell: He was from a newspaper background.

Captain Van Ness: Yes, and if I remember, I believe he was doing a lot of the PR and getting stuff out to the people, but I don't remember enough about it.

Paul Stillwell: Did you have some internal means of publicity also?

Captain Van Ness: Well, at the reviews.

Mrs. Van Ness: Here's one of the things. Dan Armstrong. I don't know where all the others are, but this is Captain Freeman, isn't it?

Captain Van Ness: Yeah, that's right.

Mrs. Van Ness: This is Dan Armstrong, and these are his regiment, you know, in the background. They got the "E." I know you always got one when you had the—

Captain Van Ness: What are some of the others?

Mrs. Van Ness: Well, this is the commendation.

Captain Van Ness: Oh, that's something else.

Paul Stillwell: What was the "E" awarded for?

Captain Van Ness: For the best company, you know, and that would cover all kinds of things at the end of the training program, you know, everything.

Paul Stillwell: Were there award ceremonies in connection with the graduations?

Captain Van Ness: Oh, yeah, that's what this sort of thing was about.

Paul Stillwell: Were the families of the recruits welcomed, encouraged to come visit?

Captain Van Ness: Oh, yeah, yeah, yeah.

Paul Stillwell: Was this just at the graduation, or could they come other times as well?

Captain Van Ness: They could come other times, and they would meet in the recreation center. We had dances there, you know, things like that, and we arranged with the people down in Chicago to bring girls up, you know, dances.

Paul Stillwell: I would think part of the way that you would try to cut down on the VD problem would be to provide wholesome alternatives for recreation. Were they steered toward USOs or things like that?[*]

Captain Van Ness: Well, we relied on black groups in Chicago to supply the girls. I don't remember now who it was, but we had a pretty close working relationship with the city of Chicago, as a matter of fact, a lot of cooperation with them and with the health department, to try to work out the difficulties as they came up.

---

[*] USO – United Services Organization is a group of U.S. civilians who put on entertainment programs for service personnel and provide hospitality for them in many parts of the world.

Paul Stillwell: What would be your biggest satisfactions and your biggest disappointments from the work at Camp Robert Smalls?

Captain Van Ness: Well, I think probably as a general statement, I think they left the Navy better as a group than when they came in. I would like to see, if I had anything to say about it, and I don't—I would like to see the higher echelons in the social strata of the black community take more real interest in the ones that were farther down the ladder. I cite as an example at one of our board meetings at the foundation—

Paul Stillwell: This is the Naval Academy Foundation.

Captain Van Ness: Naval Academy Foundation. The executive director said, "We're having a problem with the blacks. They don't seem to be able to cut the mustard. There are too many of them dropping out and academically not doing well."

Paul Stillwell: Was this Admiral Loughlin?*

Captain Van Ness: Yes, that's right, Elliott Loughlin. And when I came back, I thought about that, and I called—I can't think of his last name. He's on the city council, a black on the city council, Leon. I can get it for you. And I couldn't get to talk to him. I talked to the—I'm sure it's the fellow who took his place, Jones, and I said, "We're having a problem at the academy of trying to get good-quality blacks to come in, and too many of them are not able to graduate and they're not performing as well as we would like to see them. I'd like to get together with Leon [whatever his name was that I can't think of it now] and see if we can't work out perhaps some sort of a program within the black community to help us find good people." I called at least three times. Never once got a reply.

And I think that that's my general impression that that does happen. They don't worry enough about the [unclear]. Now, they'll make a lot of grandstand plays, National Association for the Advancement of Colored People, make a lot of plays in the papers and so on, but when it gets right down to it, they don't do enough. There ought to be something in the schools to train these people about ordinary conduct each day. I don't have any children, so I don't know what happens

---

* Rear Admiral Charles Elliott Loughlin, USN (Ret.), became executive director of the Naval Academy Foundation in 1968; in 1986 he became chairman of the board, a position he held until his death in 1989. His oral history is in the Naval Institute collection.

in schools, but things that people ought to be doing for learning about everyday living and decent living and conduct and so on. It should be taught to all people, but certainly to these blacks also.

Paul Stillwell: Well, the schools are integrated, so they're getting what the white kids are getting.

Captain Van Ness: And I notice out here, I meet blacks. I'm on the board of governors of San Diego Community Foundation, and we have a woman by the name of Logan [phonetic] on that board who is black, very high caliber. I'd like to see people like that getting a message out to the ones farther down on the social ladder about how you're supposed to act and how you're supposed to talk in our society. I don't think there's enough of that. They need it. They need something other than arithmetic.

Paul Stillwell: Well, you've mentioned this satisfaction from producing individuals who are more trained, more capable. Did you get feedback from the fleet on the quality of product you were providing?

Captain Van Ness: By that time, it was pretty well along, and I had left. It was about the time of the end of the war when I was going to be going out to the Philippines. I did go out in the Pacific at the time that Admiral Nimitz asked for someone to come out, so I decided to go to lots of different bases to see what was happening.* They did, you know, a passing job. I can't say they did a good job. There again, I'm not condemning all of them, because there were some who did an outstanding job, but by and large, they did not. There again, we had companies that went out and were kept largely as black companies.

Paul Stillwell: Well, they didn't have too much choice, I think. It was done deliberately.

Captain Van Ness: Yeah. So I don't know what effect that might have had on them morale-wise. These are factors that—all I'm giving you is the bottom line. Now, what might have caused it one way or another, I don't know. Psychologists and sociologists can sit down and give you all kinds of reasons why things happen, but it's the bottom line that counts. When you go out to get a job, nobody's interested in what your background was or whether your great-great-great-great-great-great-grandfather was a slave or whatever. It's what you're doing today. What influence those

---

* Admiral Chester W. Nimitz, USN, Commander in Chief Pacific Fleet and Pacific Ocean Areas, 1941-45. In December 1944 he was promoted to fleet admiral, a five-star rank.

things might have on what you're doing today, I don't know. I don't consider myself qualified. But that's where I feel blacks, better blacks, should set a role model for these other people, go to the schools and tell them what's important to get ahead in the world.

Paul Stillwell: Well, I'm sure in many instances they do.

Captain Van Ness: I don't know. But I refer again to this city councilman who wasn't that interested.

Paul Stillwell: Well, it's hard to say whether he's a typical example or not.

Captain Van Ness: Yeah.

Paul Stillwell: Well, I would think even though during those two years from '41 to '43, you would have heard back from the fleet, either "You're doing great" or, "We need more of so-and-so," or whatever.

Captain Van Ness: Well, I don't recall enough of the details. All I can remember is the general impression. They were not particularly outstanding. But then, who knows? Maybe if they were looking at some whites as closely as they were looking at the blacks, they might say the same thing. I don't know.

Paul Stillwell: Well, we talked about that satisfaction you had of—

Captain Van Ness: I got a satisfaction out of seeing the difference between the recruit coming in and the recruit leaving, but I got that same satisfaction also for white companies.

Paul Stillwell: Sure. What were the disappointments that you experienced at Robert Smalls? What might you have liked to have accomplished that you weren't able to?

Captain Van Ness: Well, I don't know how to answer that. I can't think of anything else that I would have liked to have done. If I thought at the time—when I thought of anything that I would have liked to have done, I did it.

Paul Stillwell: So you weren't really frustrated.

Captain Van Ness: No. Disappointed that the entering quality wasn't as good as we would like to see it, but pleased with the improvement by the time they left.

Paul Stillwell: Then you said you went to Washington. What did your duties entail there?

Captain Van Ness: Well, it was the overall policy of what to do with the progress of the program. That's where the start of the officers' deal, selection of officers, began, and then there were problems all the time that you have in any operation in the Navy. You're not sitting there reading a magazine all day. There's always something happening that's either good or bad, and we had our fair share of that, too, maybe a little more than our fair share, because from time to time, there would be racial conflicts.

We wrote up a pamphlet that we put out. I wish I'd kept a copy of it, that we put out as a guide to people who had blacks coming to their command, to try to break them away from any stereotype impressions they may have had and to treat these people the same as other people were treated. When we started to distribute the blacks around, we wanted to make sure that they weren't treated any differently and that there was no Jim Crowism where they were going. We had it in recruit training, but we wanted, as much as possible, to break away from the Jim Crowism when they did leave. We did have companies that went out to the Pacific, and when they got there, they were in Jim Crow setups.

Paul Stillwell: Cargo-handling groups, for example.

Captain Van Ness: Yes, that's right. Whether it was intentional or not, they said, "Well, let's get us a cargo-handling group," and we supplied the people, so they were all black. I don't think that was good, frankly. I don't believe any of that exists today, but I don't know.

Paul Stillwell: No, I would doubt it today.

Captain Van Ness: Yeah, yeah.

Paul Stillwell: Were you involved in the setting up of the initial shipboard-manning programs by black sailors?

Captain Van Ness: Charlie Dillon had more of that assignment than I did.

Paul Stillwell: Do you have any idea who made the determination that there would be these ships, the *Mason* and a PC?*

Captain Van Ness: A lot of that was happening, you see, while I was overseas, and Charlie was handling it. I don't know the details. That's why I kind of think it would be good if you talked with Charlie.

Paul Stillwell: I hope I can do that.† Did you get involved any at all in the selection of the men who would go to these ships?

Captain Van Ness: I don't remember to what degree. I'm sure that Charlie and I would have talked about it together, but when somebody takes over, you let him run that, and you're doing another project, you see. So I don't remember the details. We had a general policy of trying to make sure that they were treated the same, as equally as other people, tried not to treat them differently, but, in a sense, they were treated differently because we don't put out a pamphlet on how to treat white sailors when they come aboard. So there was a difference. Whether that's done today, I don't know. Maybe you see as time goes on, people don't think about—hell, most people don't even remember the back-of-the-bus days for blacks and things like that. They don't know anything about that.

Paul Stillwell: Were there methods invoked to deal with people who did mistreat or discriminate against blacks?

Captain Van Ness: Well, we always tried to do those things on a quiet basis with the commanding officer and, you know, in order not to create further animosity, you know, by hanging somebody publicly, but if we had to—I don't remember anything specific right now. Charlie might. I know

---

* USS *Mason* (DE-529), an *Evarts*-class destroyer escort, was commissioned 20 March 1944. The ship's officers were white; the enlisted men were black. USS *PC-1264* was a *PC-461*-class submarine chaser, commissioned 25 April 1944. She was the other U.S. Navy ship to have a predominantly black crew during World War II. One of her officers during that period was Ensign Samuel L. Gravely Jr., USNR, who many years later became the Navy's first black admiral.

† Unfortunately, there was no interview with Dillon.

we had cases, but I don't remember details, and we always took the stand that, "Look, that's the way it's got to be, and maybe you don't like blacks, but they're in the Navy." And I claimed all the time, "No discrimination about promotion, and officers the same way. Anybody that's in the shooting war should have the same break as anybody else. I don't know what the problems are going to be in civilian life. That's not my business. But in the Navy, it's got to be everybody has an equal shake. If he passes that exam for petty officer third class, he will get promoted." But we did not have any program as they have today—what do you call that?

Paul Stillwell: Affirmative action?

Captain Van Ness: Affirmative action, which I am *definitely* opposed to, but that's only my opinion.

Paul Stillwell: Well, I would think that one advantage of making a public case of dealing with discrimination would have been similar to the thing of bringing in Joe Louis's sparring partner, that if you say that these things are not going to be tolerated, that sends a message to other people to hold off on that kind of stuff.

Captain Van Ness: Well, of course, I wasn't anxious to publicize what I was doing there, and I'm surprised, frankly, that word didn't get out in the papers, the black papers. They could have made a big deal about that if they wanted to, but I certainly didn't tell them, and apparently nobody else did.

Paul Stillwell: Well, I can see that side of it, too, that you don't want to stir up trouble. You want to avoid giving the Navy a bad image in the public.

Captain Van Ness: Yeah. But, you know, if you go back in history, things that were bad 100 years ago, I mean they weren't bad 100 years ago, are real bad today, you know. I mean, the old Navy where you keelhauled people, you know, they got stealing, you put them out on the bow sprit with a knife and a cage, and when they got hungry enough, they could cut the rope and fall in the ocean. There's a lot of things that used to happen in the history of the Navy that today wouldn't be condoned and probably the Navy's not proud of, but that's the way society handled things in those days.

Paul Stillwell: There's no question we've made a lot of progress.

Captain Van Ness: Well, maybe we did, maybe we haven't. We've got a lot more crime today than we had then too. It's like I was down in Singapore a few years ago and talking with somebody down there, and they don't have a dope problem. Well, they don't have a dope problem because if you get caught with dope, the penalty is death by hanging. You eliminate the problem. [laughter]

Paul Stillwell: That's one way to deal with it.

Captain Van Ness: That's right. And they don't have it. So I don't know whether we can be terribly proud that our system is better. May be a lot more lenient, but it's not getting necessarily the bottom-line results.

Paul Stillwell: Are there any other specific things you remember from that job in Washington, the sorts of problems you dealt with, the programs, and what have you? Did you get visits from, say, the Urban League and the NAACP while you were there?

Captain Van Ness: Well, I was involved in that, and so was Charlie a lot with Truman Gibson. Of course, Truman, being black, knew all those people. And there was a fellow by the name of White, who was the head of that thing, National Association for the Advancement of Colored People, who, incidentally, was almost white, but he was, you know, black.* So we would sit down at things like lunch together, talk about these things. Their attitude all the time was the Jim Crow, so they were never very happy about the Navy's program, but that's where I got my first inkling, though, about not all of them are—they're more interested in their own career in whatever that organization might be than really ultimately doing the best for the guy down at the bottom of the ladder. That's a strong statement perhaps, and I'm sure it would be refuted, but among those people themselves, there's a lot of friction back and forth about things, but there is in any white group too.

Paul Stillwell: Sure. Did you see measurable progress in getting blacks in the Navy during that time in Washington? Were you keeping statistics and that sort of thing?

---

* Walter F. White served as executive secretary of the National Association for the Advancement of Colored People from 1931 to 1955.

Captain Van Ness: Well, there was a gradual breakdown of the anti-feeling. People adjust to those things. Nobody today—I don't hear much of it. Occasionally you hear of racial conflict at a military activity, but not too much. But, again, I'm not there, so I can't speak with any authority. I don't know.

Paul Stillwell: I've heard that Secretary Knox was opposed to commissioning black officers, and he died within a short time after the first group was commissioned.* Did you see any change in attitude when he was replaced by Secretary Forrestal?

Captain Van Ness: Forrestal, yes, because he set up a committee which was made up of admirals and captains, and a lieutenant commander by the name of Van Ness was the recorder. [laughs]

Paul Stillwell: Oh? What does the former lieutenant commander Van Ness recall of those meetings?

Captain Van Ness: [laughs] All I know, if Lieutenant Commander Van Ness didn't bring up anything, nothing happened, because they had other fish to fry, these admirals and captains.

Paul Stillwell: Well, were the meetings just about blacks in the Navy or about other things?

Captain Van Ness: No, about blacks.

Paul Stillwell: You set the agenda, then?

Captain Van Ness: Well, I would have to think up what we were going to talk about and what our problems were and how to handle it and, you know, get them to tell us how to handle it, but I can't be specific because I can't remember anything about that.

Mrs. Van Ness: Well, you were right on top, you know.

---

* William Franklin Knox served as Secretary of the Navy from 11 July 1940 until his death on 28 April 1944. James V. Forrestal served as Secretary of the Navy from 19 May 1944 to 17 September 1947.

Captain Van Ness: I could tell you this. The members of that board, it wasn't their most enthusiastic assignment. [crosstalk with Mrs. Van Ness]

Mrs. Van Ness: No. [laughs] [unclear].

Captain Van Ness: The general impression I can leave with you, you know, they weren't—I can see why, you know, they're not interested in that. A war was going on, you know. They didn't want to get involved with all the complex social things.

Paul Stillwell: Do you remember who was on that board?

Captain Van Ness: No.

Paul Stillwell: Was this created after Forrestal became Secretary?

Captain Van Ness: Yes, yes, Forrestal did it. I had completely forgotten about that till you brought it up, see, but, no, he's the one that did that.

Paul Stillwell: Do you remember any of the specific types of issues that would come before the board? Would there be housing situations or—

Captain Van Ness: You know, I just can't.

Paul Stillwell: I wonder if your records from those meetings exist somewhere in the Bureau of Personnel now?

Captain Van Ness: I don't know. I'm very disappointed I couldn't find my report that I wrote after I came back from the Pacific. I thought sure I had it now.

Paul Stillwell: I hope it turns up.

Captain Van Ness: Well, if it does, I'll send you a copy of it, because I—*

---

* Apparently it did not turn up, so it is not available for this oral history.

Mrs. Van Ness: You wrote it to Denfeld, didn't you?*

Captain Van Ness: Yes, as a matter of fact, Admiral Denfeld told me, "Don't send your reports through routine channels. I want you to write to me direct." So he was very conscientious about making sure that there wasn't cover-ups about anything that were bad, and I told things just like I found them [crosstalk with Mrs. Van Ness] bad in one or two places, too.

Mrs. Van Ness: Maybe if you know where the papers are, maybe they're in his papers.

Paul Stillwell: Well, that's possible, yes.

Mrs. Van Ness: That's the reason I [unclear].

Paul Stillwell: What were the things that you caught some heat about?

Captain Van Ness: Well, I recall that in Hawaii that the—and I won't remember his position, but somebody high up, a captain, called me in along with the man who had command of Aiea Barracks, and I was very friendly with the man from Aiea Barracks and I liked him, but I had to tell what I saw was wrong that could have brought on a riot condition, and, of course, nobody wanted any criticism about a race thing.

Paul Stillwell: Certainly didn't want a riot.

Captain Van Ness: No, they didn't want a riot, but they didn't want to have any kind of criticism written up about maybe they were doing something wrong race-wise that would—everybody was always talking about Eleanor Roosevelt's program, you know, that sort of thing, and they were afraid how it might affect their career or whatever.† And I know that they had this meeting, which I wasn't happy about because I had the captain staring at me—I was a lieutenant commander at the time—and I had this other guy staring at me, and I forget what he was, lieutenant commander

---

* Rear Admiral Louis E. Denfeld, USN, was Assistant Chief of the Bureau of Naval Personnel. He later served as Chief of Naval Personnel from 1945 to 1947 and as Chief of Naval Operations, 1947-49.

† Eleanor Roosevelt was the globe-trotting wife of President Franklin D. Roosevelt. She was interested in promoting opportunity for African Americans.

or commander, and here we had been friendly, we drank together, went out to dinner together. And I wrote my report. In that particular case, I gave a copy to them, but I sent it direct in to the bureau.

Paul Stillwell: What conditions did you find there?

Captain Van Ness: I don't recall exactly, but there was poor policy about something, and I don't remember what it was, things that tended to make them feel that they were being discriminated against, and you didn't have to have much to make them feel that way, because they had a chip on their shoulder all the time, so any little slight thing would upset them.

Paul Stillwell: Did you interview both blacks and whites to get these views?

Captain Van Ness: Oh, yeah, which was hard to do too. I mean, you had to be careful. You're talking to the blacks, you don't want them to think that Washington's on their side and to hell with the other people. There was a lot of things that were involved. But there was some criticism in my report, and I don't remember what it was. The only reason I remember it now is that they called me in and faced me with "what you wrote in your report," but I didn't hide it from them. I wanted them to know what I thought was wrong.

Paul Stillwell: It's interesting that people were interested in doing the right thing mainly because the effect it would have on their own career.

Captain Van Ness: Well, you know, that's my analysis of it. Maybe I was wrong, but I think it's right.

Paul Stillwell: Well, most people climbing the Navy ladder did keep their finger on their numbers. [laughs]

Captain Van Ness: That's true, yeah.

Mrs. Van Ness: That's the reason you didn't—you know, what's that man from Chicago? He got a certificate of merit or something? You know, you didn't get it. You were doing all the work for the blacks, and he was a civilian worker, wasn't he?

Captain Van Ness: I don't remember that either.

Mrs. Van Ness: That man on the South Side of Chicago. What was his name?

Captain Van Ness: You don't mean Truman Gibson?

Mrs. Van Ness: Truman Gibson.

Captain Van Ness: Well, yes. [chuckles] Yeah, he was a very capable guy, but, now, here running the black program for the Navy was a lieutenant commander and lieutenant, and running the black program for the Army was an Assistant Secretary, Truman Gibson. You know, gives you a lot more clout in your dealings with people.

Paul Stillwell: Did you have any dealings with Admiral Nimitz personally?

Captain Van Ness: No, no, I think his chief of staff, Austin, I believe, at the time was the one that I reported to.*

Paul Stillwell: Bernard Austin?

Captain Van Ness: Yeah. Yeah, I think that was it. Yeah.

Paul Stillwell: So he was the go-between? He would report your findings to the admiral, presumably?

Captain Van Ness: I don't remember now. I never saw him after I first reported in. All I did was give him or make sure they knew what was going on, but I'd still send my stuff directly to Admiral Denfeld.

Paul Stillwell: Did you get any reaction from Denfeld on what you were sending him?

---

* In 1944 Captain Bernard L. Austin, USN, became Admiral Nimitz's assistant chief of staff for administration. The oral history of Austin, who retired as a vice admiral, is in the Naval Institute collection.

Captain Van Ness: Well, when I got back, no, everything was favorable. What he did with it, I don't know, you know. I have no idea. He was not critical. In fact, he was just the opposite.

Paul Stillwell: He was encouraging you to be candid and open with him?

Captain Van Ness: Well, the trip was already over.

Paul Stillwell: Oh, I see.

Captain Van Ness: At the beginning, yes, to this extent, that he said, "Look, I want you to tell me things just like they are. Write to me direct." So he wanted to know what the facts were, and I suppose with his rank, he knew if something was wrong, people like to cover it up, you know.

Paul Stillwell: Where else did you go besides Hawaii?

Captain Van Ness: I went to Espíritu Santo and I went to New Guinea and Bougainville, Treasury Islands. That was an interesting case. Treasury Island was right across from—I can't think of the name now, Shortland Island, some other island like that, where the Japs were, and the Japs were always trying to get the planes to come over there so they could shoot at them, you know. Anyway, we landed there. I was supposed to make my tour, had a lot of blacks there, and it was mainly a kind of supply base. They put me down on the beach in a Quonset hut all by myself [laughs], so I was sleeping there with my .45 and my carbine because I figured maybe some of those Japs would come across the channel, you know.*

One night it was just raining to beat the band, and heard somebody running down the wooden steps they had there over the sand, banging on the door, and said, "Say, they want you up here right away."

Well, it turned out that, see, they worked 24 hours a day there, and they were feeding people 24 hours a day. One of the blacks had stabbed another one, and, of course, for a legitimate reason: the guy stepped in front of him in the chow line. [laughs] So he killed him. [laughs]

Mrs. Van Ness: Isn't that terrible? [laughs]

---

* A Quonset hut is a semi-cylindrical metal building that can be shipped to an advance base area and erected quickly.

Captain Van Ness: Do you understand what I'm talking about? [laughs]

Paul Stillwell: That delayed his meal even more.

Captain Van Ness: Well, the good thing about it was, I was supposed to leave the next day, and they said, "Well, gee, we'd like you to stay around and get a report on this, because the commanding officer was all upset. I don't want any hullaballoo back there in Washington about one of my blacks got murdered."

Mrs. Van Ness: [laughs] [unclear].

Captain Van Ness: You see, the thing they were always thinking about. So I said, "Well, all right." So they put some chief pharmacist's mate on the plane instead of me. He was going back to the States on leave. Well, I got down to—I think it was New Georgia I was going to, or someplace. I got there and the fellow said, "Gee, did you hear about that plane that crashed on Vella Lavella?"

"No, what about it?" That was the plane I was supposed to be on. I think one or two survivors, and they were very badly burnt. I would've been on that plane.

Paul Stillwell: So that stabbing saved your life.

Captain Van Ness: That's right.

Mrs. Van Ness: Right.

Paul Stillwell: Can you draw any generalizations about the conditions as you went farther west? How well were the blacks fitting in? How well were they being treated?

Captain Van Ness: Well, in general, I thought that they were treated all right, and I say that because I can't be specific on anything to the contrary. I do know there's a fellow now, he's about 80 years old, and he calls me. He finally made lieutenant commander, and he always says he'd never made lieutenant commander if it hadn't been for me, because at the base where he was, he had charge of this company of blacks, and he wanted it run just like we told him. "We want a fair shake for everybody." And there was an officer there, a regular Navy officer senior to him, who was making life miserable for him, you know, with the idea sort of that this officer was a "nigger lover" type of thing. And he felt that he wouldn't have made lieutenant commander except for the report that I wrote about it, because he was doing a good job.

Paul Stillwell: That he was carrying out the Navy's objectives in good faith?

Mrs. Van Ness: He [unclear].

Captain Van Ness: He got in a fight with the commander. I don't remember the details, but he let it be known that I was ruining the Navy and things like that, you know.

Paul Stillwell: What was the name of this man you're speaking of?

Captain Van Ness: I don't remember his name.

Mrs. Van Ness: Well, the younger officer.

Captain Van Ness: Oh, the younger one. Pick Baldwin, E. L. Baldwin, I remember him well.*

Paul Stillwell: He's the one that was doing a good job?

Captain Van Ness: Doing a good job, yeah.

Paul Stillwell: Are there any other specific instances you recall from that trip, other than the stabbing that you've mentioned?

Captain Van Ness: Well—

Paul Stillwell: Did you use the same technique in each place—go in, observe conditions, talk to people?

Captain Van Ness: Yes.

---

* Lieutenant Erwin L. Baldwin, Supply Corps, USNR.

Paul Stillwell: And then write up your report?

Captain Van Ness: Yeah. Mainly observing and asking questions, you know, things like that, and trying not to be too obvious one side or the other, you know, trying to act neutral, but you could generally see right away whether there was a problem there, just from things that they might be doing with the troops or whatever.

Paul Stillwell: If you saw problems, did you try in any way to correct them?

Captain Van Ness: Oh, yeah. I would there get together with the officer in charge, as I did with this particular commander, you see, who resented it right away.

Paul Stillwell: Did they in some cases seek guidance from you on what the policy was?

Captain Van Ness: They would always ask, yeah, yeah. Well, you know, even though you're a lieutenant commander, you're from Washington, you know. You're representing Admiral Denfeld. Your orders read that way.

Paul Stillwell: And you're reporting on them, too, so you've got some clout there. [laughs]

Captain Van Ness: Oh, yeah. Yeah.

Paul Stillwell: When did this trip take place in relation to the end of the war?

Captain Van Ness: Let's see. I started out on June the sixth. I remember that because on the train across the country, I heard about the landings at Normandy.*

Paul Stillwell: So that was 1944.

Captain Van Ness: 1944. And I came back; it was Election Day in November.

---

* D-Day for the Allied invasion of France at Normandy was 6 June 1944.

Paul Stillwell: When Roosevelt was reelected.[*]

Captain Van Ness: Yeah.

Paul Stillwell: How did you spend the remainder of the war after that trip?

Captain Van Ness: I went to Washington. I was going to be transferred to Subic Bay, and something happened there. I never did find out what it was, but the finger of criticism was pointed at me, and I never did—nobody told me that was the reason I was being transferred. I said, "I'd like to know what it is. If it's something bad, then, rather than be going off like this, I'd rather have a court-martial, whatever it is."

Well, somebody did something or said something, and I know at the end of the war, I had command of the officer separation center at Great Lakes, and at the end when I was getting out, they asked me to fill in. "What would you like to do if you're recalled to active duty?" and all that. In fact, Vice Admiral Carpender was trying to talk me into staying on active duty, and I told him, no, that they'd kicked me out once and there'd be another time when they'd find out I had bad eyes, even though they knew it.[†] When they decided to cut down, they'd kick me out again. So I said, "I don't want to go through that."

But what was it I was thinking?

Paul Stillwell: You were talking about some criticism had been leveled against you.

Captain Van Ness: Yeah, and I don't know what it was, never did find out. I started to say, one thing I said in that final thing they asked for, "If I'm recalled to active duty, I'll take any job, any assignment, only I don't want to have anything to do with running a black program." So you know my mental attitude at that time, because you were walking between two jagged edges all the time. It didn't make any difference what you did; the blacks didn't like it or the whites didn't like it. And I know my roommate at the Naval Academy told me that there were classmates of mine that hated my guts because I was promoting blacks in the Navy. You know, that sort of

---

[*] President Franklin D. Roosevelt defeated challenger Thomas E. Dewey on 7 November to earn a fourth term. He was not able to complete the term, because he died on 12 April 1945.

[†] Vice Admiral Arthur S. Carpender, USN commanded the Ninth Naval District, based at Great Lakes, from 3 January 1944 to 31 August 1945.

thing. So with that in mind, you knew that all the time somebody was throwing darts at you, particularly when you went out and you're off on a trip like that and you're saying something. Just like that particular high-ranking officer in Hawaii, he's got friends back in Washington, too, you know. "Get rid of that goddamned lieutenant commander," you know.

Fortunately, I got to the West Coast and stayed there, never got over to Subic Bay. I knew the war was ending, too, and about that time I got promoted to commander. So in one way I got kicked in the pants, and the other way I got a promotion.

Paul Stillwell: Was any of that resentment ever expressed to you face to face?

Captain Van Ness: In a polite way, you know, except sometimes like as I mentioned that commander. He wasn't polite at all.

Paul Stillwell: No, but I mean your classmates.

Captain Van Ness: No, I've never had any, but my roommate told me that. There are a lot of things people say that they don't say to your face.

Paul Stillwell: What sort of job did you have on the West Coast as the war was ending?

Captain Van Ness: Nothing. I waited there for transportation.

Paul Stillwell: There were several months between November of '44—

Captain Van Ness: I don't remember when it was I left. I was in Washington, you see, and then I wasn't transferred immediately.

Paul Stillwell: Oh, I see.

Captain Van Ness: I was back in Washington for some time before I was transferred.

Paul Stillwell: What else did you do in Washington?

Captain Van Ness: Same stuff I'd always been doing, you know. But then I got the—oh, I know what. I had never taken any leave throughout the entire war, never took any leave, and when I came back from the Pacific, I'd been going at a real rapid pace because there was lots of territory to cover. And when I got back, I was having night sweats, I was nervous, all that kind of stuff. I said, "You know, I think I'd better try to get some leave." So I took two weeks' leave and we went up to Wisconsin to go fishing, and it was while I was gone that these orders were issued. And to make it worse, they couldn't locate me. I should have given the address, you know, where I was and all that, but there was a real coolness about something. So whatever somebody said, it was effective. Nobody told me what it was.

Paul Stillwell: Do you think that the night sweats might have been a manifestation of nervous tension or pressure?

Captain Van Ness: Yeah. Well, it was. To me, it was pressure all the time because I'm not the type that likes to live in an environment of animosity or anything, you know. I want to get along with all of them. But it begins to tell on you, you know, year after year, you know, that you're kind of an odd character, people calling you a liberal and whatever, and you're not. You're just doing the job that they gave you to do.

Paul Stillwell: Did you do any special studies or reading in black history or culture as part of this program?

Captain Van Ness: Oh, I did, but I don't remember. You know, there was what's-his-name, that Swedish—

Paul Stillwell: Myrdal.[*]

Captain Van Ness: Myrdal wrote a book, and I think I read or skipped through a lot of that thing. Lots of people had lots of theories, you know, and blacks would have one, whites would have another, and you still have that same thing today. We have now people in this country telling South Africa how to lick their problem, but we had it in—

---

[*] Swedish economist Gunnar Myrdal did a study titled *An American Dilemma: The Negro Problem and Modern Democracy*, funded by the Carnegie Foundation and published in 1944. It subsequently came out in revised editions and had an influential role in U.S. racial relations.

Mrs. Van Ness: We still have it.

Captain Van Ness: —the '50s and '60s. We would have resented terribly to have South Africa or anybody else tell us how to solve it.

Paul Stillwell: Norman Meyer told me that the Myrdal book was very influential on him, and it was a result of that that he sought the assignment in command of the *Mason*.[*]

Captain Van Ness: Well, I got his letter and read it, and I don't have the same feeling about it as he does. I still say they were mediocre. Again, I qualify it by saying of course there were good ones, real good ones, but from what little I heard, and this is only hearsay, I do not base it on real facts because I did not get involved in that *Mason* program, what little conversation I can recall is that the ship didn't do an outstanding job. I read the stuff that Norm Meyer sent me, sounds like they had commendations coming in from all over the world, and that may be true that they did get those commendations, but what I heard was they were mediocre.

Paul Stillwell: Well, he said that he relieved a guy who was not a good skipper.

Captain Van Ness: I think to the best of my recollection, that is true, which could have set the stage for all kinds of mediocrity, you know, people when morale is bad.

Paul Stillwell: Well, he said that what the crew really needed was better leadership than it had been getting and that he set out to provide that, and when he did—

Captain Van Ness: I believe he did, because Norm is a conscientious person.

Paul Stillwell: And when he did, the performance came up.

Captain Van Ness: Unh-huh.

---

[*] Lieutenant Commander Norman H. Meyer, USNR, was a Naval Academy classmate of Van Ness. In 1945 Meyer commanded the destroyer escort *Mason* (DE-529), which until then had white officers and a black enlisted force. Meyer brought aboard the first two black officers. Meyer's oral history is in the Naval Institute collection.

Paul Stillwell: He had the feeling that his crew was what might have been expected in a comparable ship with a white crew at that time, some good, some bad, some in between.

Captain Van Ness: Well, now, he was there, see, and I wasn't. All I had was hearsay.

Paul Stillwell: So did you get out of the Navy then almost as soon as the war ended?

Captain Van Ness: No. When the war ended, I had plenty of points, so I immediately went on back—in fact, that day is when I was promoted to commander, and then I picked up and left to go back to Chicago, and I went to Great Lakes, where I was ordered for separation.* The district personnel officer ran into me and he knew me, and he said, "Don, would you stay on? We need somebody to take command of the officer separation center."

I said, "Well, I'll do that," because it would give me a chance to get my feet on the ground. I took that job and stayed on until December 31 of '46, I think it was. I got out. I had three months' leave coming, accumulated leave. I had more than that, had much more than that, but I got out to take advantage of my leave. I actually was terminated as of December 31 of 1946.

Paul Stillwell: So you spent more than a year after the war ended.

Captain Van Ness: Yeah, at the separation center. Actually, that was the most favorable job I ever had because, first place, I got commendations. The enlisted separation center, which was a huge operation compared to ours, was getting all kinds of flak from the papers, and we were getting a lot of praise, but the reason we were getting the praise was that I changed the system, you see. I didn't do it by the book. The Navy typically gets out about 8,000 pages of instructions on how to do everything, and most of it is unnecessary. I had it so that I set up a program myself, I worked it out just like I did the scheduling for the recruits at Camp Robert Smalls, set up a procedure, and I wanted it so that if somebody got there in the morning, they would be out by the afternoon. Well, at the enlisted separation center, it was taking them two weeks. So Vice Admiral Carpender ordered me over to the enlisted separation center, which had a captain as the commanding officer, had a captain as exec, and he sent me over as a commander.

** For the demobilization of the U.S. armed forces after World War II, the services had a point system to determine individual priorities for leaving the service. Points were awarded for length of service, overseas service, battle stars, decorations, and dependent children. Those with the highest number of points were the earliest discharged.

Paul Stillwell: To tell them what to do. [laughs]

Captain Van Ness: And how to do it. And usually those things don't work out. [laughter]

Paul Stillwell: I can imagine.

Captain Van Ness: So I had a whole list of things. I worked at it real hard, spent a whole day, I think two days. I went through and I saw the things they were doing that were just red-tape stuff that was unnecessary, and I wrote it up. Had a meeting with the two captains, and sure enough, not a one of those things that I recommended would work. They were working at my place, but they wouldn't work over there.

So I went back. One day I got a call from the chief of staff, and he was mad. He said, "The admiral just found out that you're not over at the enlisted separation center."

"Well," I said, "I spent two days over there, and turns out that everything that I'm doing over here doesn't work over there."

"Well, we want you to go back. You go on back there and you get that thing lined up."

I said, "If I have to go back, I'll get out."

He says, "You can't get out."

I said, "Why not?"

He said, "You signed a paper to stay on."

I said, "I didn't sign any paper." And I didn't. They thought I had, but I hadn't. And so later I heard from the admiral's aide the chief of staff went in and told him that, and the admiral laughed like hell. [laughs] And that's when he called me up and wanted me to stay in the Navy.

But I can't think of anything else to add to what I've already said.

Paul Stillwell: Did you encounter any of the black officers during your service?

Captain Van Ness: No. You mean up there at Great Lakes?

Paul Stillwell: Well, at any time.

Captain Van Ness: No, I didn't.

Paul Stillwell: Well, there were very few of them, so it's not surprising.

Captain Van Ness: I don't remember now, to tell you the truth. I don't even remember where they went.

Paul Stillwell: Well, a few stayed at Great Lakes, some went out to the Pacific, some went to small vessels such as tugs and yard oilers.

Captain Van Ness: Yeah, but I don't remember.

Paul Stillwell: One of them went to the *Mason* and served with Norm Meyer.[*]

Captain Van Ness: Yeah. Yeah, there was. There was one warrant officer I know, a black warrant officer that later committed suicide.

Paul Stillwell: His name was Charles Lear.[†]

Captain Van Ness: Yeah. He was a good man.

Paul Stillwell: Where did you have contact with him?

Captain Van Ness: Well, at Great Lakes. I mean, I knew him. He's one I recommended, you know, to become an officer. I didn't have any decision as to what rank or anything he would be, but he was an outstanding man. Like I said, you know, there were some really good ones.

Paul Stillwell: Do you remember anything specifically about his qualities?

Captain Van Ness: Well, just like about any other person. He had good leadership, good common sense, you know, somebody that you respected.

Paul Stillwell: And from what I heard, he was very dedicated to the Navy.

---

[*] Ensign James Edward Hair, USNR, was a member of the Golden Thirteen; his oral history is in the Naval Institute collection. In 1945 he became the first black officer in the destroyer escort *Mason*.

[†] Warrant Boatswain Charles Byrd Lear, USN, was a member of the Golden Thirteen. He died shortly after World War II.

Captain Van Ness: Well, I don't know to what degree, but I thought highly of him. There weren't any of them that were commissioned that I didn't think—you know, that I had anything to do with it, that I didn't think highly of, but not all of them came to Great Lakes.

Paul Stillwell: That's right.

Captain Van Ness: Yeah.

Paul Stillwell: Well, anything else you want to put on the record?

Captain Van Ness: No.

Launched in 1969, the U.S. Naval Institute's award-winning oral history program is among the oldest in the country. Used in combination with documentary sources, oral histories offer a richer understanding of naval history through candid recollections and explanations rarely entered into contemporary records. In addition, they help depict the atmosphere of a particular event or era in a manner not available in official documents.

The nonprofit Naval Institute accomplishes its history projects through contributed funds and gratefully accepts tax-deductible gifts of all sizes for this purpose. This support allows the Institute to preserve the life experiences of today's service men and women so they may enlighten and inspire future generations.

For information about opportunities to underwrite Naval Institute oral history projects, please contact the Naval Institute Foundation at 291 Wood Road, Annapolis, Maryland 21402; by phone at (410) 295-1054; or by e-mail at foundation@usni.org.

Index to the Oral History of
Captain Donald O. Van Ness, U.S. Naval Reserve (Retired)

Armstrong, Captain Daniel W., USNR (USNA, 1915)
   In World War II commanded segregated Camp Robert Smalls at Great Lakes, Illinois, including the officer training program, 5, 7, 17, 22

Baldwin, Lieutenant Erwin L., SC, USNR
   In 1944 Van Ness commended him for carrying out Navy directives on the leadership and employment of black sailors, 37-38

Boxing
   As punishment of black sailors for use of knives at Great Lakes, Illinois, during World War II, 7-8

Bureau of Naval Personnel (BuPers)
   Assignment and evaluation of black naval personnel in 1944-45, 2, 25, 27-35
   Issued a pamphlet guide for commands receiving black sailors, 27
   In 1944 dispatched Van Ness to the Pacific to see how black sailors were performing, 2, 25, 32-41
   As Secretary of the Navy in 1944, James Forrestal set up a committee of senior officers to deal with the issue of blacks in the service, 31-32

Camp Robert Smalls
   Site of segregated recruit training at Great Lakes, Illinois, for black enlistees in the Navy in World War II, 2-23, 26-27
   Punishment of black sailors for use of knives during World War II, 7-8
   Venereal disease, 8-9
   Recreational facilities, 18, 23
   Availability of chaplains, 19
   Commendations for good performance, 22-23

Carpender, Vice Admiral Arthur S., USN (USNA, 1908)
   Commanded the Ninth Naval District, based at Great Lakes, in 1944-45, 40, 45

Darden, Captain Thomas F. Jr., USN (USNA, 1921)
   In 1944 was chief of planning in the Bureau of Naval Personnel, 2-3

Denfeld, Rear Admiral Louis E., USN (USNA, 1912)
   As Assistant Chief of the Bureau of Personnel in 1944, directed Van Ness to send him reports on racial conditions in the Pacific, 32-36, 39

Dille, Lieutenant John F. Jr., USNR
   Reserve officer who was in charge of training a battalion of black recruits at Camp Robert Smalls during World War II, 14-15, 22

Disciplinary Problems
   Punishment of black sailors for use of knives at Great Lakes Naval Training Center during World War II, 7-8
   Race riot at Aiea barracks in Hawaii in 1944, 2, 25, 32-34
   In 1944 one black sailor stabbed and killed another in the Treasury Islands, 36-37

Forrestal, James V.
   As Secretary of the Navy in 1944, set up a committee of senior officers to deal with Navy racial issues, 31-32

Gibson, Truman K.
   Civilian lawyer who served during World War II as an advisor to the Secretary of War on racial matters, 11, 30, 34-35

Great Lakes, Illinois, Naval Training Center
   Construction of many new facilities to accommodate the influx of recruits in World War II, 5-6
   Segregated training of black recruits at Camp Robert Smalls, 1941-43, 2-23, 26-27

Kauffold, Ensign Vance A., USNR
   Reserve officer who was in charge of training a battalion of black recruits at Camp Robert Smalls during World War II, 14

Lear, Charles B.
   Member of the Golden Thirteen who was made a warrant boatswain in 1944 and committed suicide following World War II, 46-47

Loughlin, Rear Admiral C. Elliott, USN (Ret.) (USNA, 1933)
   Served for many years as executive director of the Naval Academy Foundation, 24

***Mason*, USS (DE-529)**
   Destroyer escort that operated with a black crew in World War II, 43-44, 46

Medical Problems
   Venereal disease among black sailors at Camp Robert Smalls during World War II, 8-9, 20, 23
   Van Ness experienced nervousness and night sweats in 1944 following a long trip to the Pacific, 42

Meyer, Lieutenant Commander Norman H., USNR (USNA, 1935)
   Van Ness classmate who commanded the destroyer escort *Mason* (DE-529) with a black crew in 1945, 43-44, 46

National Association for the Advancement of Colored People (NAACP)
   During World War II visited Camp Robert Smalls at Great Lakes to monitor the training of black sailors, 10

Representatives visited the Bureau of Naval Personnel in 1944-45, 30
In the view of Van Ness, did not do enough to help black youths, 24

Naval Academy, U.S.
Difficulty getting enough capable blacks to become midshipmen, 24

Nelson, Dennis D. II
As one of the first black naval officers, was involved in a remedial reading program for recruits at segregated Camp Robert Smalls in World War II, 16-17

Nelson, Lieutenant Commander Roger E., USN (USNA, 1921)
At the beginning of World War II, commanded recruit training at Great Lakes, Illinois, 3-4

News Media
During World War II, black newspapers covered training at segregated Camp Robert Smalls, Great Lakes, Illinois, 19-22, 29

Nimitz, Admiral Chester W., USN (USNA, 1905)
In 1944 was concerned about a race riot in Hawaii, 2, 25

Ninth Naval District Headquarters, Great Lakes, Illinois
In 1945-46 Van Ness was assigned to the district headquarters to muster officers out of the service following World War II, 40, 44-46

Pearl Harbor, Hawaii
Race riot at Aiea barracks in 1944, 2, 25, 32-34

Promotion of Naval Officers
When Van Ness reported for active duty in 1941, he learned that he could apply for promotion to lieutenant (junior grade), 2
Failed attempt to spot promote Van Ness in 1944, 2-3

Racial Issues
In the spring of 1942 the Navy began accepting black sailors in general service ratings, 4-5
Training of black sailors at segregated Camp Robert Smalls, Great Lakes, Illinois, 1941-43, 2-21, 26-27
Remedial reading training for black sailors, 6, 16
Assignment and evaluation of black naval personnel in 1944-45 by the Bureau of Naval Personnel, 2, 25, 27-30
As Secretary of the Navy in 1944, James Forrestal set up a committee of senior officers to deal with the issue of blacks in the service, 31-32
In 1944 a race riot in Hawaii sent Van Ness to the Pacific to assess conditions for black sailors, 2, 25, 32-41
Van Ness believed that top black citizens should help those less able, 24-26

Recruit Training
    Segregated training of black sailors at Camp Robert Smalls, Great Lakes, Illinois, 1941-43, 2-23, 26-27
    Some instructors and chiefs came through the Tunney program, 9-10

Richmond, Lieutenant (junior grade) Paul D., USNR (USNA, 1942)
    Reserve officer who was in charge of training a battalion of black recruits at Camp Robert Smalls during World War II, 14

Treasury Islands
    In 1944 one black sailor stabbed and killed another in the Treasury Islands in the Pacific, 36-37

Tunney, Lieutenant Commander Gene, USNR
    Headed a World War II program for physical instruction and leadership in the Navy, 9-10

Turek, Lieutenant William, USNR (USNA, 1926)
    In World War II was in charge of recruit training at Great Lakes, Illinois, 5-6, 11

Van Ness, Captain Donald O., USNR (Ret.)
    Civilian experience before being called to Navy active duty in 1941, 1
    Duty from 1941 to 1943 at Great Lakes Naval Training Station, 2-23, 26
    Served 1944-45 in the Bureau of Naval Personnel, assigning black sailors and evaluating their performance, 2-3, 25, 27-42
    In 1945-46 was assigned to the Ninth Naval District headquarters at Great Lakes, Illinois, to muster officers out of the service, 40, 44-46

Venereal Disease
    Among black sailors at Camp Robert Smalls during World War II, 8-9, 20, 23

www.ingramcontent.com/pod-product-compliance
Lightning Source LLC
Chambersburg PA
CBHW080609170426
43209CB00007B/1379